"To create order out of chaos is what the poet achieves at his best. In a kind of Wildean preface, a one-paragraph manifesto, Stimac states that he views his "role" poetical as a mosaicist. Isn't this the call of good poetry? This claim is well stated by this poet. Chaos is what we are. Language is part of the mess we are in, the part over which we have most control. As a friend of mine Charles, an anthropologist, said, "Art is communication." I really think much poetry these days skips over that verity. Stimac has something to communicate, with a love of language and a measure of control, these poems take history into account. This book will comfort and inspire."

-C. Srygley-Moore, *Termites Amidst the Milky Way*
(Kung Fu Treachery Press, 2022)

"Richard Stimac's beautiful *Bricolage* gathers objects lost, uncovered, unearthed, and remembered and, reencountering these relics, asks "for what good?" Why remember? Why revisit? Memory, Stimac says, "demands we act." These poems are themselves acts in the vein of John Clare: observing, praising, and aching. Stimac has redeemed these lost wrecks, bottle shards, old dolls, and distinctively American landscapes with formal acuity, simultaneously precise and inventive. *Bricolage* is a delight."

-Stephen Frech, *Into Night's Tent*

"Stimac's book is a collection of things, experiences, tiny places that evoke feelings about the Rust Belt. *Bricolage* reminds me of the different time and century we live and die in now, of the desuetude and tragic damage everywhere. What remains for us are fragments of our past. Stimac has seen it all with an ophthalmologic eye and delicately transmutes his desolate and choking world into his work. His art is expressed so colorfully, full of kairic moments of satori and inspiration. His vehicle is the sonnet driven out of the English poetry garage and made new again. It's perfect for hammering out our past, forming it into our future, turning our gift of rust and ruin into his sublime poetry."

-Seven H. Bridgens, *The Hobo Bob Cantos*

(OAC Press, 2022)

"Richard Stimac has woven together a collection of the tiniest treasures and moments of life— from a boy trying to make "stone walk on water " to yard sales where the bargains "make their value known." These remembrances ring true for all of us. He asks us to reconcile an authentic life out of the shards of what has been left behind by the years. Stimac travels through the mysteries of a childhood faith, weaving in a history of time and place——the pieces of life for which we have no choice but to eventually confront."

-Diane Vogel Ferri, author of *Everything is Rising*

Bricolage

Poems by Richard Stimac

Spartan Press

Spartan Press

Kansas city, Missouri

www. spartanpress.com

Spartan
Press

My thanks to the following faculty at Southern Illinois University at Edwardsville:

- Edmond Jacobitti led me to the history of ideas.
- Stanley Kimball taught me to write.
- Sheryl Meyering helped me finish a published paper on Willa Cather.
- Brian Abel Ragen introduced me to contemporary formal verse.
- Eugene B. Redmon showed how to live as a poet true to personal experience and larger literary traditions.
- Fred Robbins allowed me to sit on the student editorial board of *Sou'wester* and see how the sausage is made.

Beyond Words "Ties" (as "Ties that Bind"); *Burningword* "Waste"; *Clackamas Literary Review* "Repossessed"; *december* "In Memoria"; *Faultline* "Wildflowers"; *Havik* "Confession", "Night Prayer", "Still Life", "Terminal", "Visitation"; *Limited Experience Journal* "Elodea"; *The Examined Life Journal* "εσωσεν αλλους"; *Michigan Quarterly Review* "Mermet Spring, Illinois" (as "Calument Springs, Illinois"); *Mikrokosmos* "Kish"; *Mom Egg Review* "Visiting Mother Jones's Grave (Union Miners Cemetery, Mount Olive, Illinois)"; *Moonstone* "Articulation"; *New Plains Review* "Shadows"; *NOVUS* "Bricolage", "Goodwill", "Hardened Tears", "Tread softly . . . "; *Passengers Journal* "Arabia"; *Penumbra* "Demobilized"; *Talon Review* "Harvest-tide"; *The Road Not Taken* "Infinite Limits"; *Salmon Creek* "Chain of Rocks"; *The Stillwater Review* "Trespassing"; *Wraparound South* "Artifacts", "Bonne Terre Mine"; *Wingless Dreamer* "Rest"; *The Write Launch* "Salt", "Skipping Stones"; "Like a foolish man".

Jim Ott chose "Visitation" for third place in the *Havik* 2021 Poetry Contest.

A.E. Stallings chose "Kish" for second place in the *Mikrokosmos* 2022 Poetry Contest.

Contents

I always imagined my role as a poet like a mosaicist. I take small, often uneven pieces, scraps, refuse, and, gently, precisely, with caution, arrange these disparate tesserae of stone, glass, ceramic, brick, porcelain, cement, marble, terracotta, pebbles, sea shells, smalti, maybe even material seldom used, like wood or coins, or cork. Anything solid but incomplete can be contained in a greater whole. Close up, the brokenness is obvious. Alone, a chip is worthless. Who values a chard of busted beer bottle? We sweep up the remains of yesterday and hide them in plastic bags and metal trash cans. But in patterns, even the dregs we toss into landfills becomes art. From a distance, fragments of the past gain an illusion of solidity. If we take time to notice the insignificant, the wreckage, the detritus, the pain and the happiness, both we are too willing to forget, then we will find the elements to create the present from the past. What we name as today is, forever, a construct of leftovers, a slowly dissolving remembrance, saved from oblivion. To remember is to be.

-RS

I dedicate this book to my mom and dad, my brother, my grandparents, my aunts and uncles, my cousins, and all those who I grew up around. I come from good people.

Solo una cosa no hay. Es el olvido.

"Everness" Jorge Luis Borges

Time present and time past
Are both perhaps present in time future,
And time future contained in time past.
If all time is eternally present
All time is unredeemable.

"Burnt Norton" T.S. Eliot

Skipping Stones

The skipping of stones
depends on choosing
water-smoothed stones
cradled in thumb and forefinger
(it's more the flick of the wrist
than the whip of the arm),
only to watch in amazement
silky, thin stones
dance, then disappear
beneath concentric, transverse ripples,
awe our leaden efforts
could not crack petrified laws of nature,
could not make stone walk upon water.

Achelos

Let's take the metaphor of rivers, deep
and calm. Where they will lead us? We may know
the strength of currents and of undertow,
how rivers, sometimes, seem to rest, asleep,
whose jealousy, revenge, wrath, sends cold shivers
through interred veins of lead and coal that flow
like frozen streams no ferryman can row
our souls across. Oars tear and snap to slivers
on outcropped rocks that break the long-held tension
that separates the water from the air.
Where does, indeed, earth, air, and water end?
Which angelic way leads us to ascension?
Where do we face when given whole to prayer?
Where is the river on which we transcend?

American Steel

She staked claim between the flood and the flame.
Her daddy burnt their trailer. Better ash
than foreclosure. No one treat them like trash.
After that, the last unemployment claim
ran out. Momma took her home. No one blame
her for that. Then daddy died in the crash,
drunk, God damn him. Momma would wail and gnash
her teeth. In truth, she'd say, he died of shame.
Broke his soul more than his body, the mill
did, when it close down. But he always thought,
her too, something was owed them, no, not owed,
stolen, outright, something they owned, that showed
they was meant to be, not just sold, and bought,
owners, too. Someone has to pay that bill.

Arabia

One thousand miles upriver from Algiers,
five hundred more from Memphis and Cairo
where barges forge the meager Ohio
through locks and dams and rusted winding gears,
past where the brown Missouri disappears
into the Mississippi undertow,
they found *Arabia* in an ox-bow
dry bed of fallow farmer's fields. For years,
I paid to see the wreck, the China plates,
tinned meats, the guns to stanch the flow of blood
from Kansas, cylinders that cymbal crashed
like sunlight across sand, and, unabashed,
I saw self-reflections, as if the Fates
chose me as ground upon which they would flood.

Articulation

Confess your secrets in the prose of touch.
I will hold them in the palm of my hand,
pour, grain by grain, into my mouth, like sand,
each unspoken word that you cleave and clutch
so close to your unvoiced body with such
a will even the ground which you still stand
upon melts into a featureless land
without echo. Your silence is as much
present as absent. So I read your skin,
closed eyes, a finger on each bone, each crest,
line, facet, process, fissure. In each novel
articulation a virtue, a sin
you whisper with lip, thigh, arm, back, and breast,
your voice, dust in which a sinner would grovel.

Artifacts

Near Horseshoe Lake, Cahokia's plotted site
collapses, mound by mound, from inside out.
The river's down from what it was, the fight
gone out of it. Still, even in this drought,
the archeologists reconstruct, piece
by piece, the skeletons of priests and kings,
all under pressure to stop work. The lease
is up soon. No one can pull the right strings.
The past depends on laws the state enacts
each year. The world sinks, soft silt beneath us.
A viscous earth, words, buried, artifacts,
shards our heirs will unearth, debate, discuss,
brush, ossified, hardened, like Midwest soil.
Remembering is apart from God's toil.

Ash

Iron ore, at thirteen hundred degrees,
sinters with coke and flux and pours and steams
into torpedo cars. Hot metal seas,
like melted sand, apocalyptic dreams
of vanquished beasts and celestial strings,
of ladle, tundish, mold, shroud, glass lakes, streams
of molten earth, return whence they came. Things
are more what they were than they now are.
From smokestacks, as if filled with God's breath, rings
of kish ascend, more beautiful than star
or moon, like ashen air, enshroud the town.
Streets glimmer, pale, thin, like a faded scar.
This body, this ground, this earth, must fall down,
ash to ash, dust to dust. With breath, we drown.

Bargains

The beautiful are found in discount crates,
or folding tables in driveways and front yards,
or simply set on the curb. Fractured plates,
reclining chairs with bum legs, a deck of cards,
missing the Queen of Hearts, board games, stained clothes,
rust-caked tools, shoes with worn out soles, the shards
of tossed memories of someone who knows,
now, the things we mistake for life are trash.
I like to hold that I'm a man who chose
differently. I'm not. More confused than brash,
I buy other's rummage, make it my own,
a balance of cast-off pasts. It will crash.
All life does. Love, too. Both need to be thrown
out, then reclaimed, to make their value known.

"Behold, the Lamb of God, . . ."

The haunts of my childhood persecute me:
the Security & Trust, now bankrupt;
Croatian Home's lamb spit, rusted, swings free;
St. Agnes, suppressed, foundations corrupt,
past repairs, demolished as urban blight.
The echoes of dead children's cries disrupt
my peace. Now, with what conceit do I write
about abuse? What trope, figure of speech,
metaphor, symbol? No, nothing is quite
as should be. I am mute. Words cannot reach
the past, down halls never passed, a locked door
never opened. The undone echoes breach
my soul, my parts, the frame, the wall, the floor,
ghosts of bodies I will never restore.

Blooms

The springtime blooms carry a bitter scent:
New shorn grass turned to mulch, frothed fringetrees,
red cedars, after ice, snow, and wind bent
their trunks like sacrocants bowed at the knees.
Each May, they live, again, but, then will die.
Why is that? In damp afternoons, no breeze
begins to blow. No Lord walks, with a sigh,
begs of my disobedience. My years,
have no divine equinox. God, I cry,
who does not wonder? All too human tears
water fallow fields. My sole breath, the cold
winter wind. My only harvest, my fears,
perennials, petal by petal, fold,
wilted, dried, rotten, prophesies, foretold.

Bodies

I hung a fading photo on my wall,
my great-grandparents, on their wedding day,
with somber, smileless eyes filled with dismay
more so than joy. A hand-knit silk lace shawl
around her waist, the bride surveys the hall,
a dream of beer and smoke that bleeds away
before her. Disappointed, she will stay.
In time, my grandma would try to recall
a bitterness bequeathed to her, and then
my mother, in turn to me. Like mysteries,
I see reflections of the groom and bride.
They stare, like burnt icons. Again, again,
the past holds shape. The dead have not yet died.
We bear, inside us, all our own histories.

Bonne Terre Mine

Missouri hides its truth in two extremes.
You can see, down the blue State Highway K,
past where the land proceeds to shift from clay
to rock, near Bonne Terre, with its active seams
of surface-stripped lead, roaring monstrous teams
of earthmovers that scrape, day after day,
the overburden laid above the gray
ore veins. The spoilage dumps in crystal streams
that snake past dogwood, willow, elm, and ash,
then weeps down walls of dissolved limestone caves,
or, merged with rivers, discharges in the sea.
This refined land, its beauty and its trash,
All we love, and debase, sinks in these waves.
Yes, we sink, too, and figure ourselves free.

Book of Knowledge

In the TV room, a partial set, lying
flat on a dove-tailed rude applewood bookcase
my grandpa built, nurtured my child's undying
desire to know it all. Things in their place,
branches of science, roots of words, would plant,
in me, folios, volumes, one by one,
save the missing "I." So sure nothing can't
not be, each known fact memorized, so none
escaped me, I became knowledge. Without
me, the world did not exist, me, who ruled
the indivisible, to live beyond doubt,
in an imagined paradise. So, fooled,
too many things, too little of time, life grew,
past dry, marginal fields I never knew.

Bricolage

My mom reconstructed our lives from junk.
Unbleached cardboard Orisha beaded masks,
glass-shard mosaics of proud Mary's face,
a twisted crown of bottle caps and barbed wire,
found relics, littered our tar-paper house,
each *objet d'art*, a fetish, meant to stave
the shame of being poor. We ate, each night,
on painted plates of resurrecting suns.
She formed so much what others tossed away.
Now I scrounge through *virtu* and bric-a-brac,
the scattered trifles of remembrances,
to find her, traceless, gone. My soul sets bare,
Unfit to curate memory. I house
no rags, no cracked cups, no heart, fit for pawn.

Cahokia

Thoughts of loss envelop me when I pass
slumping Monks Mound. The now more common rain
softens the quick clay, unearths the long grass.
Beneath? Junk: shards, flint, ash, splinters, spent grain,
crushed bone. Just one mile away, Midwest Waste
mounds plastic, metal, glass, rubble, remnant vain
lives, buried, denied. And what of me, chaste,
Smug, but, hidden, afraid to die, to be
disremembered? My sin is my pain placed
in selfish darkness. Who will exhume me,
brush dust off thought, desire, fear, tagged, glassed,
for onlookers to peruse, for a fee,
caress, fondle, weigh, in their soft palms, massed
rare fossilized flesh, a tangible past?

Calm Before

I slept through most of the late afternoon
while driving rain and wind tore limbs from trees
and downed telephone lines. Leaves and trash strewn
the streets. The air, thick, except when a breeze
carried a light touch, like springtime, pushed downward.
Now, I was awake. A siren's reprise,
then another, and a garden flowered
in my mind. I could see sound and hear sight,
as if each of my five senses devoured
each other. I fear my mind is not right.
I long for the time before sleep, the blest
time, before the storm, even before night,
when there was only day, no task too pressed,
no storms, no loss, no sin, no need for rest.

Chain of Rocks

A chain of rocks cleaves the river in two.
In spring floods, the hidden peaks can wreck
a flat keeled barge, crew scattered on the deck,
one man, fore, fallen in the swirling slue,
beyond the wake. In June drought, trash will strew
the granite: Igloo coolers, tires, long-neck
Bud bottles, a fridge, a bed, all scrap and speck
of lives some one of us made, used, then threw
out. Sometimes, I walk on that water, stone
beneath my feet, bearing me just above
the bent current. I fish for scraps, the past,
artifacts, relics that proved what we love,
though tossed into memory, is not cast
adrift, the past be something we can own.

Confession

We shoved on monkey bars, the steel slide,
chain swings, through sewer pipes, the best for hide
and seek. You showed me yours. I showed you mine.
Ten years, same place, we'd drink our Mad Dog wine
and wrap ourselves, like relics, side by side
and count risen stars. That was good. Wide-eyed,
I rudely kissed you down your neck and spine.
They always warned us not to cross "the line."
Some Sundays, Mass concluded, the priest
and families returned to their homes, we'd feast
on flesh, too, flesh of arm and thigh and breast.
In my bedroom, a confessional booth,
we mocked and shrived each other's sins. In truth,
condemned to death, unknowing, we were blessed.

Congregation

You were my sweetened sacramental wine,
my raised unleavened eucharistic host.
Your essence laid on my tongue. Your divine
mute form stamped my sheets. Your holy ghost
took breath from my soul. Remember, again,
that season was no ordinary time,
but Passiontide, for you to come, amen,
unveil the icons when Sanctus bells chime.
But, now, it is done. Time takes what time lent.
I lose my faith. Idolatry returns.
Plaster gods squat in the temple. Curtains rent.
My bed, empty, I am a slouching whore.
I mock God's forgiveness. The city burns.
You abandoned me. I will love no more.

Demobilized

My dad left parts of himself in Viet-
nam. You can see them in a tourist pic:
a foot under a tea house table; a rick-
shaw decorated in red ribbons for Tet
holds forearms in the spokes; a girl, baguette
a femur's length under her arm, skips quick-
ly past a begging monk; a snapped chopstick
gives the finger, angry at unpaid debt.
These are keepsakes no one meant to amass.
The collector of these gems is a fool.
Another father, ARVN, VC, N
VA, amputated names from a time when
names mattered, sits in the shade on a stool
and counts his own parts scattered in the grass.

Depth

The rules were writ in red on a white card
with this prophetic warning: "No lifeguard
on duty." Kids swam as parents saw fit.
Beyond the stained deck chairs, mothers would sit
in daylight hours, with lotion, ID card,
room key, TP, Band-Aids, cash. It be hard
not to find what you need, when you need it.
At night, the hotel pool was bottom lit.
Come midnight, when doors were locked, lobbies still,
when no one, except us, would stir the pool,
beyond the fence, the light, the known, the fact,
we'd tread water, silent and bare. The thrill
of breaking rules, of playing the wise fool,
submerged, made us innocents in our act.

Dispossessed

Composed of bricks and cinder blocks and boards,
each abandoned building sings its own song.
A paraclete wind rattles dry casement stays,
whistles through splintered blinds, shudders slate roof tiles.
Wood frame, stone, sheet metal pitches, intones
tales, fables, yarns, secrets, sometimes lies, in strong
twangs, whispers, cries, calls, or swaying low moans,
the cadenza lament of a tacit phrase.
Once, eyes closed, I listened to a hushed blaze--
a home groaned, sighed, breathless, in a fire storm--
heard flame-tongued angels, among ember piles,
sing disjointed melodies, harmonies, chords,
God's fallen cadence, and, silent, in His praise,
collapsed in grief. There is no rest in form.

Elodea

Your mother died too soon, as mothers do.
With her, a part of you was set adrift,
to float the Russian steppe, its rivers, swift,
the Tom, the Ob, until the Artic, blue
and clean, the frigid current pulling through
to America, promise, threat, and gift.
Like water plants your parents would cut, lift
from mud, you would root. This we know is true.
I wish I were your mother, to lay you
to bed at night, to lift you up at day,
to braid your hair, to smooth your silken dress,
to walk with you through wide purple pansy fields,
and tell you fairy tales that wash, like rain,
the tears away, deep sadness, deeper pain.

Embrace

The last slow song that ends each night is soft
in its embrace and scents of gentle touch fall
upon the floor like stars that hung aloft
in now dark skies. Like day, the lit dance hall
forgives no one. Dawn has fallen on all.
We thought our human bodies could be doffed
and rouge and tie and dress and speckled shawl
would cover our shame, somehow, would forestall
the foretold death. Then the stars saw us, grinned
at our ambition. This is why we dance:
to forget we are lost, are not at one
with ourselves, but, if, only, by willed chance,
we could undo the loss that had been done,
could make a time, a place, where none had sinned.

Empty Fields

Fields, fallow, empty all year, fill the space
between my old hometown and weed-run tracks.
The idled mill furnace, empty docks, and stacks
of creosote ties give no hint, no trace,
that once the rivers and railroads, a lace
of water and of steel, conveyed crates, sacks,
books, boots, rifle, shot, chattel, sickle, hammer, axe,
New England chairs, Jamaican rum, a vase,
Italian, for a St. Louis *salon*.
Besides these sterile furrows, I saw no
goods, though, faint, heard stilled rails hum a blues song
for what could have been. The hand-forged, too, long
for lost time. Makers are the last to know
when manufactured worlds break. All is gone.

εσωσεν αλλους

"He saved others"

(Matthew 27:42)

My father carried Agent Orange in his bones.
My mother bore a cancer in her womb.
But, with sweat, he brought forth bread from stones.
She rocked through nights in a sick child's room
and turned her face to a silent, empty sky.
He cursed the earth, whose dust would be his tomb.
At night, in bed, I'd hear them talk, and cry,
but with the risen sun, they made a bearable life
for me and my brother. Who thought they would die?
I could not command my father, "Stand. Abandon strife
and sin no more." Or stanch my mother's flow
with a touch more precise than a surgeon's knife.
Whence could I save them? I did not know
to save myself. How can I repay what I owe?

"Even angels long to look into these things"

Mary of Czestochowa's icon, massive,
maternal, watched over the parish poor
with eyes enclosed in gold-gilt tiles, cold, passive.
Mass said, Father would charm, as much as bore,
us with his words of love, forgiveness, grace,
that echoed with submit, obey, adore.
With folded small hands beneath each small face,
we'd genuflect, cross ourselves, wait our turn,
endure the priest in his dark, shriving place.
Now, even now, his eyes, his breath, his yearn
for my salvation, that mute, stillborn weight,
sin, unforgiven, as if I could spurn
God, turn my back, bend crooked what was straight,
form mortal, divine, mouth choice, deny fate.

Focal Point

Near the abandoned trolley loop, inside The Focal Point,
where melodies twist like strings of light
and rhythms rest in the tongue and groove joint
of suspended dance floors, couples reel right,
then left, hover, angels before a flame,
enamored with the fretlessness of dance,
trills, runs, slurs, legato, no praise, no blame,
no choice, no consequence, no God, no chance.
I watch from outside. Coming? Going? Yes,
aren't they the same? My reflected face stares
at me, fragmented, between what I see,
what I am, or could be. Stress lies on stress.
Time, in my mind, silent, a line— in pairs,
choice, unchoice, as one— forms us, bound, and free.

Frosted Pane

A frost had blurred the pane. I could not see
beyond reflections in the glass, opaque
with fractured ice and shrouds of feathered flake.
The splintered sill stained deeply black as tea,
and blinds half-drawn, kept the small room draft free
from bitter cold. Yet, I felt a hard ache
glide through my marrow, numb, as if the snake
had taken me, by mistake, as the tree
that fell in that God-forsaken dark wood.
Or so I imagined my ice-bound twin
reflected back to me. The dim-lit mirror
had brought us face-to-face, and for what good?
For no salvation, no forgiven sin,
nothing brought closer, not hardened, not clearer.

Frozen

The Mississippi froze from side to side.
The current, still below, continued on.
It can't refuse the sea, to what it's drawn,
to empty silt conveyed southward from wide
and fallow plains. There's pics of those who tried
to cross the ice on foot one cloudless dawn.
Their shadows bridged the banks. That day is gone.
Last winter, someone I loved, too much, died,
in embrace, crystallized, transparent, still,
in thought. Ephemerally formed, God's breath
will thaw. It's trite, but life depends on death.
And memory, to be, demands we act.
However tightly ice or love is packed,
there's movement underneath, against our will.

Goodwill

The re-racked tops, bottoms, frocks beggared us.
Remember, bodies, once, possessed this cloth,
my mom reminisced. When we took the bus
past bodegas, the hot-press mill, the swath
of storefront churches, tarpapered shotguns,
a land of corrupting rust, engorged moth,
to purchase, for the next fall, clothes the nuns
found fitting, we, too, made out like a thief
at night. She dressed me like the rich man's sons,
and gave herself, yet attained no relief,
Cried out, "Come, Jesus!" Where, then, was the Lord?
Without memory, one can have no grief.
Now, she is dead. My loss, my pain, I hoard
indulgence even beggars can afford.

Hardened Tears

We'd walk the rails and search for beads of glass—
jade, amber, puce, lapis— frosted and rough.
You told me they were the tears of trains shed
for passing all the sadness of the world.
Who knew sadness fit in a palm? At home,
in bed, we held those hardened tears to light
and saw, in each, the loss, the pain, the death,
heard the engines heave, the whistles lament.
I've kept one, tucked in my chest, where I save
those few things I love. On sleepless midnights,
eyes closed, I roll, like a relic, that stone
across my cheek, as if it were your touch
set to calm my blind fear. But you are gone.
I cannot cry. My tears, too, have grown cold.

Harvest-tide

A Madonna and Kit-Cat Clock, both nailed
on Grandma's kitchen walls, each, its own saint,
birth and death, kept watch, lest the leaven failed
to rise, borscht, no more boil. Her gentle plaint,
mild, as she worried a rosary bead,
would waft, like incense, sweet, and stale, a faint
forecast. She'd let her garden go to seed.
She cellared no canning after this fall.
I went, when she called unto me, to read
my face, then spread a salve of wine and gall
across my chest. That winter, next, she died.
I hear her, still, slip-shod, scuttle down the hall,
to knives, dulled, pots, black, burdens, set aside,
the doors, locked, oven, cold, floors, swept and dried.

Heavenly Bodies

White jet trails demark the blueprint-hued sky.
Right angled infinite parallel lines
create new horizons above the dry
perspective. Of the earth's too small confines,
we delineate heaven. With desire,
soon, planets will subdivide into plats
and dry moon seas will assess for acquire
the subdivision of hard tidal flats.
Yet, here, on my small plot of clay, I wait,
and measure time, itself a sort of place,
a point I blocked, or saved, or had a date
with that someone, who, I can't recall the face,
but knew I was in love. That's why I recount
days, weeks, months, years. Space must hold some
    true count.

"I ain't sayin' you ain't pretty"

I admit dumbest thing I ever done
was let that man give me a wedding ring.
I always saw love like who lost, who won,
saw me as loser. Still, there ain't a thing
I'd take back. Sure, I had my girlish dreams.
Oh, writin' poetry, or join a band,
or maybe goin' back to school. It seems
there's some things I do miss. I wanted land,
a place my own, and make as I saw fit,
paint the walls, I don't know, yellow and pink,
and not care what he thought. Not care one bit.
Oh, God, oh, man, it all gone in the blink
of an eye. Welp, have me a cigarette.
Ain't no good comes from worry or regret.

"If you do well, will you not be accepted?"

Did my duty, serving in the last war.
Back home, skipped the G.I. bill, went to work,
the swing shift, moving my way from dock clerk
to warehouse boss. Who thought there could be more?
My faithful wife, love her. Kids I adore.
My church. The buddies. Never one to shirk
a job. Yet, in shadows, I see sin lurk
and wait for me to stumble beside my door.
Always thought myself more than able to master
whatever burdens God placed on my back.
I believed work, and success, was a grace
that saved us all from that dark past disaster.
Life's mundane weights uncover what I lack.
I am ungrateful. Christ, I hide my face.

Infinite Limits

The rails confined my home. The trainyard guards
patrolled the right of way and swung their jacks.
At night, my parents crashed, beyond the tracks,
the chain link fence, cracked concrete, brown, bare yards,
the shattered dreams sown like sharp beer bottle shards
from last night's drunk, alone, I'd hear the Amtrak's
sad invocation, the train's clicks and clacks,
the accented meter sung by ancient bards.
My borders made an infinite expanse.
Imagination defined my small earth.
I knew, without reservation or doubt,
I didn't deserve, by action, or by chance,
by law, decree, or chart, or by low birth,
these limits. I would work my own way out.

In Memoria

Levies breached. Incus clouds threatened more rain.
Floods drowned hard red spring wheat. Towns dissolved. Whole
roads washed away without trace. Vacant coal
mines, limestone karsts collapsed. The earth will drain
itself. I had come, not for loss, or gain,
to bury my mother. I crossed the sole
clear bridge, felt the derecho sway and roll
the superstructure in play. Life is pain.
The DOT erased the signs. I knew,
still, where to discover the displaced ground,
to rehear the same words mouthed for each dead,
to resee, like burnt icons, family shed
remarkable tears. Memory was all I found,
her presence in absence, me, lost in rue.

Jefferson Barracks National Cemetery

Death confounds me. Even more so, life. Why,
advanced from nothing, uncaused, we are born
to cold, hate, scorn, fear, loss, love, then to die,
where no one, in oblivion, can mourn?
Two-thousand-six, my mother died. Her grave
visage, chiseled in memory, here, lies
among white stones, crosshatched, as if to save
the dead from river barge wakes, steel rail ties.
On the bluffs, at the Barracks, thunder rolls
with charging rain, a flanking line of clouds.
I watch, dry, from my car. The water scrolls
through trenches of cut names. The windshield shrouds
me from beaten grass. Unshriven, I stay
til clouds retreat. Darkness gives in to day.

Jimmy

I.

When I learned he'd run, I knew, in my gut,
it was for good. My Jimmy, gone three days.
He was my friend. They found his bike, sideways,
along the tracks, the fractured frame, the strut
turned back against itself, a cracked locknut
on top a spike. Somehow. He would amaze
me, Jimmy would. In summertime, the craze
upon him, washed-out jeans, blond hair uncut,
he'd stand between the humming tracks. The train
horn wailed both to forewarn and to lament
this boy, who (for me, was both good and strong;
so I thought; I could not have been more wrong)
held his life cheap, as if already spent.
Death cradled him, in pleasure, as in pain.

II.

They moved next door when I was almost ten.
The whole town knew the dad, and the mom, drank.
We'd hear him cuss, then she would howl, "Don't yank
his arm so hard." Some nights, at supper, when
I said his name, my mom would smile with blank
eyes. My dad would say, "Fact is, to be frank,
not our concern." I know less now than then.
I'd lie in bed. The TV's ghostly glow
would dance along the walls a dance of death,
and life. A plea to heaven for respite,
(I can remember, almost, but not quite)
I would pray, cry, out loud, til out of breath,
God would admit what I knew He must know.

III.

The police found him in another state.
He'd walked that far. Teachers had to pretend
at not knowing. Cautious, not to offend,
in unsure tones, they would prattle and prate
and praise Jimmy. We knew it was too late,
at that age. In Mass, when we would ascend
the steps, kneel, give tongue to the Host, the weight
of sin, of their silence, taught me to hate,
and, how true love is, always, a bit sad.
The pain of loss, of all, prompts us to save
ourselves, stay, by imagination, blind
to inevitability of the grave,
reside in imaginary pasts, mad,
by God, this world, be, as is so, designed.

Kish

The senator stood on top the pay shack
and extolled the virtues of union dues
and voting Democrat. He held that track.
We stood in line, the midnight shift, our views
obscured by kish, lack of sleep, and the sun.
Its rays, like arms, would grasp through the night's blues,
blacks, browns, off-whites, the sky, bruised, just begun
to heal. We aspired to die in our beds.
Then rise, return whence we came, a short ton
awaiting us, retread the path, past sheds
of fading rust. The mouth, the nose, the throat,
parched, death's dust on the lip, the ashen heads
of penitents hung low. Dry prayers bloat,
then rot, then burst. He knew he had our vote.

Last Year's Cold

I don't remember last year's winter rain,
how cold made breath hurt knife-sharp and bone-deep,
how rivers jumped their banks like hoards that sweep
across the plains and bring the time of pain?
I don't recollect rummage that remain
in piles by broken curbs, a cairn-like heap,
too damaged to fix and sell on the cheap.
Too much work for too little past to regain.
At this age, even, can I have a spring?
Each winter is no death, but a short season
before one, then another, to no end.
On frosty days, the evergreen limbs fling
the snow beyond reach, toss it without reason,
not one thing to be lost or to amend.

"Let your peace return to you"

The closed interstate led me to be just
another person who didn't choose to roam,
leave one life, say goodbye to friends, to home,
to lose sense of place, shake off blacktop dust,
silent playgrounds, cracked asphalt, red rust,
empty parking lots, corner stores that tend
to working poor. Here, the shuttered mills lend
an air of judgement, loss of faith, of trust.
But who's to judge if one should stay or go,
as if "I" and "place" were the same set fact,
as if our choice of "where" formed the deep cause
of why we are, age, die? We never know
what lies beyond. Yes, I think, not to act
makes all the same end. That should give me pause.

"Like a foolish man"

The town of Kingdom stands on sinking land.
A web of railroad tracks holds things in place:
the steel works, diner, drive-in, Saving Grace
Reformed Baptist Church, itself raised on sand
of an oxbow lake. As a boy, I'd stand
on top the banks of railroad tracks and brace
against the train that even shook the space
between the sharp wheels and my outstretched hand.
The earth swayed. I could taste it on my breath,
the risk, the taunting of a seeming stable
world. It was as if the train were a knife
that cut the thread that bound me, so unable
I was, I am, to accept foregone death,
inevitable fragility of life.

"Lone and level sands"

One day, in her own time, my daughter brought
me a threadbare doll, found half sunk in sand,
the summer river low. Her tiny hand
embraced a legless trunk. The yarn hair taut
with hard mud. The black bone button eyes, fraught
with mocking. Lips, frayed and darned with a strand
of velvet cord. Around the waist, a band,
charmeuse silk, with Roman letters, hand-wrought,
with fine stitchwork, a name. What, I couldn't tell
this child, is that nothing she loves will last.
When grown, would she, then, prefer I'd lied?
I bent before her. Her shoe was untied.
She dropped the doll. We left, already past
time for her nap, for me to rest a spell.

"MENE, MENE, TEKEL, UPHARSIN"

A jealous god, my mother would fix me
against the kitchen post, her thumb blood red
with leaden paint, to mark— an unheard plea,
hand flat, pressed fingers earthward, palm on head—
my height, and, equally, to seal her dread
another year, another setting sun,
blanched, cold, then she delivered me to bed.
The room black, I watched revelations run
across the pallid walls: what's done is done,
the whispers, like ghosts, from across the floor,
soft, breathed into my ear. I've kept just one
thought, image, really: impressed on the door,
thumbprints, like sprinkled blood, as much to warn
as to appease, lest God claim her firstborn.

Mermet Springs, Illinois

In Little Egypt, near Cairo, Thebes, and Karnak,
straight along Highway 57 south,
along the current's misgiving switchback
where the river is wider than at the delta's mouth,
in an old stone pit, we've sunk our culture's wrecks:
a coal car, airplane, pick-up truck, the scrap
and waste of someone's dreams, life, foregone projects.
Our lives' ends fit so neat and clear on a map.
I pay to dive, to explore the rust and the grime.
No book, no history gives guide
to my search. I do, as you, breath, breath, in time
see, touch what the cold, lightless waters would hide.
We cast our lives in cold, wide, silent pools
of fading light. Memory is for fools.

New Madrid Fault

Near New Madrid, the earth contests itself.
An old rift undermines the soot-black silt.
Dark seas, hidden, kept, deep beneath the shelf,
will, soon, swallow the river. Levees, built
by well-meant Army Corps, will breach, and burst,
as if risen on inquisitive guilt
to test limits, quench a forbidden thirst.
I've endured my entire life on this fault.
As if, by God, I had been blest and cursed,
like the land, once sunk beneath the Gulf's salt,
tremblors shake my soul. I feel my mind split
in two. Time, space fall into the black vault
beneath consciousness. No Furies acquit
me. I shall lie in the abysmal pit.

Night Prayer

This cloudy, new moon night, the star-like lights
of grain silos and elevators shine
across the river, water black as wine,
as if constellations fell from their heights,
sky, earth, in exchange. A dry bulk barge rights
itself as feed grain mounds send up a fine
dust, and the watery stars shimmer, a sign,
that God, awoke, has put us in his sights,
or nature is indifferent. To you,
as you walk across heaven's floor, your soles
singed by seraphic heat, you turn your eyes
up to hell's glory. And me, in my fuss
for banks and cars and who leads in the polls,
I pray fallen words never reach the skies.

Promised Land

On the far edge of town sat the promised land
her mom had banked the best part of her life
on. Land her father left to his third wife,
the one he divorced. Nothing goes as planned.
Not that the land was worth much, clay and sand
and floods each spring, summer, too, when the Knife
River backed up. "The beginning of strife
is like letting out water." Her mom, tanned
and tall, and worn out, but in a good way,
in a "life well lived" way, yes, she would quote
that Bible verse, and then look her up and down,
like car buyers do. She'd furl her brow, frown,
and mumble, gasping gripped breath, then clear her throat
and say, "Water you trust. Blood you betray."

Purgatorio

I led a life as pure as iron smelt
in coke-fueled furnaces, beside the tracks
and metal sheet walls and burnt-brick smokestacks,
tar-paper shotgun shacks, where the people dwelt
who lived by rosary and beer and belt
upon their backs, ate their bread, paid their tax,
and measured years by Easter's spent candle wax.
What molded me? What impure dross could melt
within my soul to refine my mind, mill
me into kish, the grit of molten ore
cast from the depths and burst through mantle and crust?
My soul, a flamed stream, would breach levies, spill
into the sea, or rise from ocean floor
to form black sands. I, too, return to dust.

Relics

Our house butted an unsown field's turnrow
and slough of hyssop, ditch weed, scouring rush,
poison hemlock, beggar's ticks, blackthorn sloe.
During dry summers, we'd sift through the brush
for fossils, flint arrow heads, bottles of green
thick glass submerged beneath the reed and slush.
We set them, cleaned, before the window screen
and retold myths of monsters, heroes, shades
and sprits. Our bedroom became the scene
of epic wars, of shadowy charades.
And there, too, hung Jesus on his rood cross,
overseer of all. What deals and trades
we made to avoid the meaningless loss
of death's discards, with its scobs, lees, and dross.

Remembrance Day

I measured out my life in cans of beer,
weekends, playoffs, car repairs, broken dreams
I kept alive. Like my favorite teams,
I told myself there was always next year.
Back from the war, the parades, and the cheer,
made me think how all is not what it seems.
I'm not a thinker, or tend toward extremes,
so I felt more numb. Almost dead with a fear
when my daughter enlisted, deployed in turn,
I watched the news that forgot we were there.
My pension is funded, the house paid off,
I have time to brood. What I had to learn
I've already forgot. Smoke fills the air
from the mill's furnace. My eyes tear. I cough.

Repossessed

Earthmovers leveled the tract houses. Where
a grade school, now a Target. My best friend's
home, parking spaces. Mine, a shaded square
of green ash. The asphalted train track lends
a sense of evenness. Shadows not seen
will not be missed. I returned to save things:
bronzed shoes; Rosary of Mary, The Queen;
my mom's Bakelite bangles, Hobé rings.
What did I forsake? What is it I took?
Precious foreclosure, host of pawned past,
enveloped fictions, haunted facts, I leave
nothing. Nothing, I imagine, will last.
Reprised of memory, let me not grieve
like tightly veiled Lot. I refuse to look.

Rest

She lay wet and beaten on the kitchen floor.
A soup pot simmered over an open flame.
And if it should boil over, who's to blame?
Her wearied eyes looked through the open door.
A wine glass lay spilled. The table next the drawer
stood legs upright, or arms raised to proclaim,
"Glory to God!" and call mercy on His name.
Each day has its task and each hour its chore.
Like Christ on that fateful day, she arose
and brushed the snarled hair away from her eyes
and smoothed her cotton robe against her breast.
They will not wash and dry themselves, those clothes.
Tonight, she'll make supper such a surprise.
All she would need, just a little, was a rest.

Rivière du Bois

(Lewis & Clark's first camp, Wood River, Illinois)

The Shell refinery dregs percolate

through black bottom soil, deep, to flooded caves.

Koch Nitrogen tends its freight terminal

upstream. The river smolders with crude pitch.

Two hundred years before, Lewis and Clark

winter-camped here. In spring, they poled and barged

west, chartered the plains, fixed claims coast to coast.

The state rebuilt their stockade and keelboat,

and, Babel-like, a cast concrete tower

to climb, heavenward, sightsee the rivers'

convergence, the twin flows, unmixed, like time,

equal, part past, part present, tract-bound facts,

a green now, a brown then, one beside one,

til they merge into a darker downstream.

Salt

All the salt in the world comes from the sea.
That's why we tunnel under the Great Lakes,
to chip away a seabed that now flakes
beneath hydraulic steel machinery.
That's why our salty tears eternally
burn our clenched eyes. Or why the body aches,
with each step, with each breath, and trembles and shakes,
as we sweat the salt inside us. So we,
you and me, built, as far from shores, a home
where rivers run backwards when the earthquakes,
as if time reversed by divine decree.
What we took as ground was nothing but foam
that dissolved beneath our feet. The sea takes.
The sea gives. All that was will always be.

Sanctuary

With frosted hair that flutters like pennants,
the iced wind rampages through the city streets.
The trees lay bare and the grass, all brown,
as if marauders waged total war against the earth.
I wander from room to room, through the art museum, warm
by the oil-fed furnace in the catacombed basement.
Color and contour, brush stroke and angle,
points of view, and vanishing perspectives
act as a diversion for my mind in retreat
from the bitter burn without the window pane
and the heavy brass doors. Who would blame me
to hide amidst the dead masters and their artifacts?
Who really believes that in a world gone mad,
Sanity is other than restrained hermitage?

Seasonal

A cold depression brings the freezing rain.
Hard artic winds, so raw, sparrows stop singing.
I can hear their silence through the fine pane.
Clouds of frost dissolve while branches, swinging
with ice, bear, heavenward, like those who've sinned,
the weight of memory, a distraught clinging
To suffering. Even the air has thinned.
In my heart, here, in the Midwest's heart, whole
seasons migrate. Months lose form. Too thin-skinned,
I burst my confines. A guilt floods my soul.
When the sun seems to never resurrect,
my mind, plain, flat, is swept by snows that roll
like crashing waves, the salt spray, white spume flecked
across my face. What more could I expect?

Shadows

(somnium americanae)

At dawn, the Gateway Arch casts weighted shadows
westward, as both memorial and warning
to olden days. But dusk, like sagging gallows,
the shadows hang east, returned, lost in mourning
for destinies unmanifested. One
city park away, the Old Courthouse, scorning
the Arch's ideals, rejects progress. None
can deny this fact. Scott lost his person-
hood. Pulitzer bought his paper. The state done
with its case, Minor had no vote. Things worsen.
A tired dream fades. The muddied river flows,
A false promise. We thought we could immerse in
a current, history, that never slows
course. Independent, time goes where it goes.

"Silent, upon a peak"

(St. Francois ("Francis") Mountains, Lead Belt, Missouri)

I climb, too far, too steep, today, mark tree tops,
sway of green-tipped waves, distant rooftops like wooden
    ships.
The Osage called this peak Taum Sauk, highest in the Ozarks.
The French christened the entire range for St. Francis.
These are true mountains, sleeping volcanos,
once an archipelago in a transgressing salt sea
that cleaved a continent clean in two,
united arctic ice with tropical tides.
From my perch, I survey each plat, note, distant,
like a *caravela* mast, as a lead smelter's smokestack
grey signals, high, into a pacific blue sky.
Breath held, here, sunk, a wreck, beneath the drift
of indifferent time, settled on a silent seabed, I will not rise,
as if words, though writ in water, have power in the naming
    of things.

Still Life

I'd cruise my bike along the earthen levee
and watch the towboats push with or against
the current. Standing there, my boy's mind heavy
with coming, going, watching, still, I sensed
my shifting, not the laden barges' sway.
Illusions of self-motion trick us all.
We assume life fixed, that we choose our way.
Maybe my watching those shoal-draft boats crawl
ground fear in me, that dread will leads to loss
of freedom, of choice, of time held. It seemed,
fixed, calmed, the earth at rest. It's me who'd cross
from point to reciprocal point. I dreamed
of space firm, of time with no start, no end,
no sorrow, no loss, no sin unredeemed.

"Suffer the little children"

When the river fell, the slough turned to mud,
black, silky, that hardened in summer heat,
like the serrated keels of some cold blood
ancient chthonic monster. I'd sink my feet
in silt. That slush made me ready to die,
so cool, so calm. At the back door, I'd meet
my mom, flooded with rage. She'd curse and cry,
on the soiled tile floor, grieve, a bit coy,
nestle me between her legs, and with a sigh,
wash sludge from my toes. Like Jesus, with joy,
she suffered the little child. But I would wait,
to return to mud. That's what a little boy
is made of, I'd chant, mix up love for hate.
I learned to discern the two far too late.

Tagged

We called ourselves lords of that feral lot,
the unmarked field behind Benjamin Moore,
K-Mart, Kroger, the Central Hardware store.
A crisscross of dirt paths, shacks, and a plot
of straggly trees, stub branched, frail, leafless, squat,
between the stores and broken back screen door
of what was home, though how our parents swore,
fought, drank, a "home" is not the word we'd thought.
We ran like packs of dogs, me and my friends.
We tagged each other, "It!" That was the game.
There really was no clear goal. Means were ends.
Then, in time, we grew up, to each his own
path. Let's not forget what we had once known:
our power had come from our right to name.

Terminal

At airports, I always feel a bit sad.
Arriving, and departing, both, as one,
reminds me how nothing is ever done,
at least for good, and really not for bad.
When there's no more of a good-bye to add,
someone says, "Ends are something new begun."
We see, or am seen, in the setting sun
a lover depart. Who can't not turn mad
at the loss of it all? For sure, I can't.
The endings, and beginnings, so misnamed,
like terminals, combining one as two,
make me so want to hold still, God, to rant
against the sky, once so pure and untamed,
a promise I believed was wild and true.

Ties

A set of rails circled my boyhood home.
I'd lie in bed at night and dream to walk
the right of way without purpose, just roam,
past shopping mall, steel mill, and loading dock.
The mall closed years ago. The mill grew cold.
Smokestacks stand like stone keeps from Gothic tales.
The rails no longer sing. As was foretold,
the world changed. Shifting markets. Dropping sales.
Collapsing pensions. I thought the rails led
to infinite points I would one day reach,
a world without end, terminal, or grave.
Come home to lament and bury the dead,
I cross the ties that bind me and count each
to each, a past, that I could never save.

"Tread softly . . . "

Streetlights reflected off the mist-wet grass.
Like stars, each blade shimmered, as if the sky
fell, a tapestry, braided with cut glass,
Beneath our feet, silver stich, verdant dye.
"Imagine," I said, as we lay, our hands
interlaced, arms twined, backs damp, closed eyes dry,
"I wove heaven, pulled each weft taut through strands
Of warp, and set it here, for you to rest,
As I hold you tight." Then you slept. My plans,
faded like the dew, your head on my chest,
I prayed, silently, so I would not wake
you, you, who kept my words of love, be blessed.
Then night was done. Our day began to break
on us, with dry voice, blurred eye, marrow ache.

Trespassing

Near Grand, by abandoned Commonwealth Steel's
furnace, the vacant street car shed, the mound
of batteries leaching lead in the ground
water, and the ocean of rust-rimmed wheels,
me and Mom would mold junk and trash we found
into new things: comic masks, a bedazzled sock,
a cardboard cathedral with glass and rock
rose windows. A trash bag kite! With the wound
string taut, slack, taut, slack, the kite would balk, mock
us, helpless, then crash, return whence it came.
Steadfast, my mom held firm: no one's to blame.
We'd climb through the chain-link fence, walk the block
back home, across tracks, to our daily bread,
and pray for forgiveness and grace, then bed.

Troubled Water

I crossed that bridge, but, then, again, came back,
and stood along the railing. Swirling pools
and eddy lines demarked the river's tack
against itself. We all return, like fools,
from where we came. The source tugs us.
We give. Unseen currents, unspoken rules,
towed me to stand above the iron truss,
granite piers. If I dropped my wallet, keys,
shoes, untied, then, calmly, without a fuss,
released myself over the bar, with ease,
and slipped, a miracle, into the brown
slurry, my bronzed arms flailing in the breeze,
what troubling angel, kept from work, would frown,
wings drawn, turn away, tightly wrap its gown?

Via Dolorosa Memoriae

Arranged, in rows, mats neatly set between
them, dozens of girls, throats bound, or skulls crushed—
did any of these soon dead primp or preen—
lie, buried, one thousand years, until brushed
immaculate. And this was just one mound.
The earth flowed red in Cahokia. Hushed
a century, other bones, still unfound,
in East St. Louis, smoldered in burn pits.
White mobs burnt street after street to the ground.
These graves, ten miles apart. Now, the Arch sits,
bow-legged, westward. Removed, as I am,
to finger a map that, with blues, greens, grits
against my skin, as if progress, a sham,
who, who asks, does the past presume to damn?

Visiting Mother Jones's Grave

(Union Miners Cemetery, Mount Olive, Illinois)

Incus clouds change hues: soft coal to hard lead.
Lightning strikes. Furrows flood with summer rain.
Beneath these plains, a cross of empty mines
supports the country's heartland. My car whines
down gravel country roads. The tires throw stones
and shake off dust. And there, a wailing train.
I've come to try and honor bygone dead.
They buried Mother Jones in Mount Olive.
A cracked obelisk marks her resting place.
No flowers grace her tomb. She will not rise.
I ache for her faith in progress. But lies,
here, history, yet unseen, fills this space
around her grave. "Her boys" no longer live.
None will unearth these wrathful Irish bones.

Wager

He took the train to play the River Queen.
The railroad bridge with bent-spined struts of steel
rear summersaulted right head over heel
across the brown-backed river. He played clean
through the night, one hour, two, ten, twelve, fifteen.
Rolled the red dice, saw and raised, spun the wheel,
and never took blame. It's always the deal.
The pit boss would nod. He knows what they mean.
On the way back home, tired, he saw the river
run its due course along the banks of silt,
marked each lock, each dam, each grain-laden barge
and felt the spirit inside, mute, quiver
and carry loss in streams of soft, felt guilt
that will stay booked, until time's end, a charge.

Waste

When I think of heaven, I see trash:
broken bottles, leaking Freon, used notebooks,
Thanksgiving scraps, industrial dross, ash
of lives that rot and leach into the brooks
and streams that feed the river, then the sea.
Yet, when I conceive a perfect hell, it looks
unpeopled, manicured, fresh, foolproof, each tree
equal, sidewalks flat, no black oil stain
on any gray driveway. Loveless and pure.
Why, then, am I so ashamed of my pain?
I haul my grief in my sinful junk cart,
as if I could secure peace from this vain,
broken, human life. No, I live, not apart
from death, my pardon pawned, deep of my heart.

"Whence I Came"

The plastic fish washed up along the beach,
a garbage strewn littoral thin stretch
of seaside real estate that soon would fetch
a bottom-feeding price. Rising tides breach
the grey seawall and blue-green waters reach
the second stories. Houses spew and retch
and gasp for breath like the noontime lunch catch.
When we shall drown forever without speech,
who says, I ask, were we not meant to be,
in wasteful, wanton ways, mute nature's tools,
that gas and oil and cast synthetic strands
are not in nature's plan? We may not see
what comes. Before we crawled from calm tide pools,
we lived as ignorant as wave-washed sands.

Wildflowers

Between the drainage ditch and rust-stained rails,
and the concrete bed of River des Peres,
beneath the Arsenal viaduct, where
I picked, illegally, along the trails,
wildflowers-- tickseed, asters, lizard tails,
snakeroot-- you'd sit and braid them in your hair.
No one sowed them. I figured fair is fair.
My tiny thefts would never tip the scales
of justice or of time. Who really lost?
Not us. I'd bluff a kiss, and you would hide
your face. Your arms and legs, like vines, would cling
to me. I'd lie if I said it wasn't pride,
fear, perhaps, this need to sidestep the cost
of life, and steal flowers from each year's spring.

Visitation

I've wandered into some old church
On a rundown street, the dive bar
Next door for those left in the lurch
By idled engines, empty rail cars,
Closed foundries, cold kilns, dead steel yards.
The tar-roofed shotgun shacks still blaze
With the ghosts of the refuse and discards
Of what we call the simpler days.

Simple is not what I'd call the people
Who measured weeks by Sunday Mass.
Like Uriel, set to guard the steeple,
They kept ward over broken glass,
Cracked blacktop with hopscotch crosses,
Rusted chains of bent iron hoops.
Score was kept of wins and losses.
They rocked and watched from sagging stoops.

With their mute mouths, glass eyes, deaf ears,
Like faded pastel plaster saints,
They marked and shed mortar-like tears
For coal girl's pleas, brakeman's complaints.
Who would hear them? The whiskey priest?
All he did was preach the divine.
That was something, he thought, at least,
To clear black lung, straighten a spine.

When you . . . when I, I meant to say,
Like an angel, make my visit,
Up steps, through doors, a passageway,
Maybe I will ask, "What is it
That led these poor to drop their cents
Into the plate to build this place?
What empty cupboard, past due rents
Went unpaid in lieu of this grace?"

Above the alter of gold leaf,
Mary holds a small man, Jesus,
And signs to all the way from grief,
As if seeing itself frees us
From misery. The senses save
More than the mind. They understood,
The old, who wore black, and were grave,
Life is for grief and not for good.

Historical Context

Achelos was a Greek river god. His name may be rooted in the Akkadian word for "water of the river invading land."

Agent Orange was a defoliant used by the United States in Southeast Asia. St. Louis-based Monsanto was one producer. Monsanto founded the town of Monsanto, Illinois, across the river from St. Louis. The city is now Sauget. Dead Creek runs through Sauget. At night, it glows and in the past the water has caught fire.

American Steel, Granite City, Illinois, is the successor to Commonwealth Steel. In the early 20th century, as the name implies, Commonwealth Steel had employee-ownership programs, along with a wide range of social and educational programs. Those programs ended through a series of corporate acquisitions.

Arabia, a steamboat, sank in the Missouri River in 1856. A farmer discovered the wreckage in 1988. A Kansas City museum houses artifacts from the boat.

Bonne Terre Mine is a decommissioned iron mine in Missouri's Lead Belt. The mine has been flooded and is used for recreational diving. Jacques Cousteau filmed a documentary in the mine in 1983. This area of Missouri is in ongoing EPA Superfund site.

The **Black Madonna of Częstochowa** is an icon from Poland. The icon allegedly was painted by the Evangelist St. Luke. The position of Mary is one of the *hodegetria,* "one who shows the way." Mary points towards Jesus who stands on her lap. The icon is black due to a legend of its burning yet surviving. Scholars suggests that Mary originally had Slavic facial features that had been changed to more Western European features. The icon is revered in many Slavic countries.

Book of Knowledge was a widely popular young adult encyclopedia.

Cahokia was the largest Mississippian Mound Builder city. The largest population may have reached 40,000 around 1100 CE, one of the largest cities in the world at the time. There were over 100 mounds. Some contain remains of mass human sacrifice. No evidence explains why Cahokia collapsed after a short period of time. The largest mound **Monks Mound** rises 100 feet and has a base the same size as the Great Pyramid of Giza. All the mounds were built solely with human labor.

The **Chain of Rocks** is a natural outcropping of granite creating a low-water dam on the Mississippi River between Alton and St. Louis. During the summer, when the river is low, fisherman walk into the river to reach the pools that dam creates. The Chain of Rocks Canal with a lock and dam allows rivercraft to avoid this hazard.

The **Eads Bridge** is the oldest bridge across the Mississippi River and the first bridge built below the confluence of the Mississippi and Missouri Rivers. The bridge was the first in many ways: the first to use steel for a large structure in place of wrought-iron; the first cantilever bridge; the first to use pneumatic caissons to dig through the riverbed to bedrock; the first to document "the bends" from workers ascending from the caissons. At the time, the bridge was also the longest rigid span bridge in the world. Riverboat interests in St. Louis and state laws blocked financing of the bridge and James Eads, the engineer, financed the bridge himself.

The **East St. Louis Race Riots of 1917** caused dozens if not over a hundred deaths and left thousands homeless. The result was an exodus of African Americans from the city. In 1952, Josephine Baker related in a speech given at the St. Louis Municipal Kiel Auditorium that as a child she hid in a railyard during the riots.

Elodea, also known at waterweeds, is a native aquatic plant of the Americas. It has been introduced into other continents and is considered an invasive species.

The Focal Point is a folk performance center in Maplewood, Missouri. A block away the Sutton Loop Park is a square that was once the turnaround for streetcars to reverse direction for their return from Maplewood to St. Louis.

The Gateway Arch is the tallest human-made made monument in the world. Designed by Eero Saarinen, The Arch is a stainless-steel, weighted-centenary arch. The Arch is part of the Gateway Arch National Park and symbolizes St. Louis as "The Gateway to the West." The Arch sits in St. Louis' downtown on the west bank of the Mississippi River. In the morning, the shadow of The Arch casts west, and in the evening, east.

Horseshow Lake is an oxbow lake near St. Louis. The lake is a remnant of a side channel of the Mississippi River. The lake is also a National Natural Landmark. Most of the lake is recreational, including fishing. A US Steel foundry sits on the western edge of the lake.

At the start of the American Civil War, **Jefferson Barracks** was the largest U.S. military installation. Located on bluffs south of St. Louis, the Barracks is now a St. Louis County Park, part of the local VA medical system, a national guard and reserve station, and the largest national cemetery, second only to Arlington.

Little Egypt is a nickname for southern Illinois due to the confluence of the Ohio and Mississippi Rivers, the regular flooding, and the rich soil. Cairo, pronounced "kay-row," sits on the southern tip of Illinois at the confluence of the two rivers. Memphis, with its pyramid, lies further south, while Thebes and Karnak are in Illinois.

"Mene, mene, tekel, upharsin" were the words that appeared on the wall at Belshazzar's Feast. The words can be translated as follows: "mene – God has numbered your days"; "tekel – you have been weighed and found wanting"; and "upharsin – your kingdom will be divided."

Mother Jones, an Irish immigrant, was once called "the most dangerous woman in America" due to her union organizing, especially among coal miners. In 1898, in Virden, Illinois, striking mine workers opened fire on Chicago detectives escorting African American strikebreakers from Alabama. Miners and detectives were killed and the miners won the strike. The men from Alabama continued to Chicago. Mother Jones was present and famously called the miners "her boys." Two results of the violence were the United Mine Workers Union becoming de facto segregated and Virden possibly the first sundown town in Illinois. Mother Jones is buried in nearby Mount Olive in the Union Miners Cemetery. Her monument had been in disrepair but has since been restored.

In southeast Missouri, the **New Madrid Fault Line** (**"mad**-rid") may be the most unstable fault line in North America. In 1811-12, a series of New Madrid earthquakes shook church bells in Boston and forced the Mississippi River to reverse its flow upstream. Predictions by FEMA estimate a major New Madrid quake may possibly be the greatest catastrophic natural disaster in U.S. history. Though estimates vary widely, the general range is a fifty-percent or greater chance of an magnitude 6.0 earthquake or greater in the next fifty years or less.

The **Old St. Louis County Courthouse,** part of the Gateway Arch National Park, was a combined state and federal courthouse. In 1846, Dred Scott lost his claim for the right to sue before the Missouri Supreme Court that met in the Old Courthouse. In 1872, Virginia Minor was convicted of illegally voting. The United States Supreme Court upheld both decisions. In 1878, at an auction on the Old Courthouse steps, Joseph Pulitzer bought the *St. Louis Dispatch* and merged it with the *St. Louis Evening Post* to create the *St. Louis Post-Dispatch*.

All **salt** does indeed come from the sea. All naturally occurring sodium chloride comes either directly from existing salt water or from deposits from ancient salt seas. Salt mines are not only mines into the earth but mines into what once was the ocean.

The **St. Francois Mountains,** pronounced "Francis," rise in the northeast corner of the Ozark Plateau. These mountains are true mountains originating from volcanic eruptions, as compared to the Ozarks Mountains, formed by displaced plates. Two-hundred-fifty to 500 million years ago, the Western Interior Sea connected the Artic region to the Gulf of Mexico. The St. Francois Mountains then were an archipelago, the only dry land in the entire waterway. Large bodies of salt water like this that encroach on land are termed "marine transgressions."

Uriel is a cherub, one of God's direct attendants. Uriel is also the guardian of the entrance to Eden. As the Angel of Repentance, Uriel is known as a pitiless and harsh judge.

Wood River, Illinois, was once owned by a French settler who named his land Rivière du Bois, after a small stream on his property. The location is near the confluence of the Mississippi and Missouri Rivers. In 1803, Lewis and Clark made their first winter camp on this land. Illinois has recreated both Lewis and Clark's stockade and their keelboat, and built a concrete tower for onlookers to note how the dark-brown Missouri and lighter-brown Mississippi flow side by side until merging further downstream. In 1814, local Native Americans killed around a dozen white settlers near Wood River. In 1917, Shell opened a refinery in the town. Today, the complex is Phillips 66's largest capacity refinery. Wood River is an EPA Superfund site.

Richard Stimac has a forth-coming poetry chapbook *Of Water and of Stone* (Moonstone) and published over thirty poems in *Burningword, Clackamas, december, The Examined Life Journal, Faultline, Havik* (Third Place 2021 Poetry Contest), *Michigan Quarterly Review, Mikrokosmos* (Second Place 2022 Poetry Contest; A.E. Stallings, judge), *New Plains Review, NOVUS, Penumbra, Salmon Creek Journal, Talon Review, Wraparound South.* He published flash fiction in *BarBar, Flash Fiction Magazine, New Feathers, Paperbark, Prometheus Dreaming, Proud to Be* (SEMO Press), *On the Run, Scribble, Talon Review, The Typescript,* and *The Wild Word.* He has also had an informal readings of plays by the St. Louis Writers' Group and Gulf Coast: Playwright's Circle, plays published by *Fresh Words* and *The AutoEthnographer,* and an essay in *The Midwest Quarterly.* A screenplay of his is in pre-production. He is a reader for Ariel Publishing.